IT'S TRUE!

THIS E
IS BUGGE

D1112934

Other  titles

Pigs Do Fly
Terry Denton
PICTURES BY Terry Denton

Crime Doesn't Pay
Beverley MacDonald
CARTOONS BY Andrew Weldon

We Came From Slime
Ken McNamara
PICTURES BY Andrew Plant

There Are Bugs in Your Bed
Heather Catchpole and Vanessa Woods
PICTURES BY Craig Smith

Your Hair is Dead
Diana Lawrenson
PICTURES BY Leigh Hobbs

Hauntings Happen and Ghosts Get Grumpy
Meredith Costain
PICTURES BY Craig Smith

An Octopus Has Deadly Spit
Nicki Greenberg
PICTURES BY Nicki Greenberg

www.annickpress.com/microsites/itstrue.html

SUE BURSZTYNSKI

PICTURES BY MITCH VANE

IT'S TRUE!

THIS BOOK
IS BUGGED

annick press
toronto + new york + vancouver

To Max, Amelia, Dezzy and Rachel,
with love from Auntie Sue

Copyright © text Sue Bursztynski 2007
Copyright © illustrations Mitch Vane 2007
Series design copyright © Ruth Grüner 2007

Annick Press Ltd.
First published in Australia by Allen & Unwin.

Proofread by Audrey McClellan
Production of this edition by Antonia Banyard
Cover photograph: Comstock (spy) and
Rebecca Ellis / iStock.com (dragonfly)
Set in 12.5pt Minion by Ruth Grüner

Cataloging in Publication
Bursztynski, Sue
It's true! this book is bugged / by Sue Bursztynski ; illustrated by Mitch Vane.

Includes index.
First published in Australia under title: It's true! your cat could be a spy.
ISBN-13: 978-1-55451-080-1 (bound)
ISBN-10: 1-55451-080-5 (bound)
ISBN-13: 978-1-55451-079-5 (pbk.)
ISBN-10: 1-55451-079-1 (pbk.)

1. Espionage—Juvenile literature. 2. Spies—Juvenile literature. I. Vane, Mitch.
II. Bursztynski, Sue. It's true! Your cat could be a spy. III. Title.

UB270.5.B87 2007   j327.12   C2006-906205-6

Printed in China

1 3 5 7 9 10 8 6 4 2

Published in the U.S.A. by   **Distributed in Canada by:**   **Distributed in the U.S.A. by:**
Annick Press (U.S.) Ltd.   Firefly Books Ltd.   Firefly Books (U.S.) Inc.
                                    66 Leek Crescent   P.O. Box 1338
                                    Richmond Hill, ON   Ellicott Station
                                    L4B 1H1   Buffalo, NY 14205

Visit our website at: www.annickpress.com

CONTENTS

WHY SPIES?

Spying is the world's oldest profession, in existence ever since one tribe needed to know what the other tribe was doing. Men, women, and children have been spies. During World War II, the Jews of the Warsaw Ghetto in Poland were fighting the Nazis, who wanted to murder them. Children and teenagers often made their way in secret through the sewers to find out information and bring back weapons needed by the fighters. A boy called Baruch Bursztynski rode a bicycle rickshaw as part of his disguise. One day, he drove a Nazi passenger who had no idea that he was sitting on top of a pile of weapons! Although many spies and agents didn't survive their missions, Baruch did. He grew up to become my dad!

S. Bursztynski ☆

WHO IS
THIS MAN?

1

SNEAKY SPiES
AND GREEK
GiFTS

Spies live in a dangerous world.
Their job is to find out enemy
secrets and bring this
information back to their
leaders. They could be
killed if they are caught,
so they often wear a disguise or go
undercover and live among the enemy.

Spies have to be very careful and very cunning. In ancient times, soldiers made good spies and so did travelers because they could go from city to city.

There is a story about King Alfred the Great, ruler of Wessex, in Britain, over 1000 years ago. Alfred thought he might do some hands-on spying. The Danes had invaded his country, so Alfred disguised himself as a wandering minstrel and cheekily went to the Danish camp. He played his harp and sang love songs while the Danish leaders were meeting to plan their next battle. Did anyone in that tent wonder about the singer sitting in the corner playing beautiful music? We'll never know. But Alfred won the battle.

Alfred was a real king, but this story may be a legend, like the legend of the Trojan War.

THE TROJAN WAR

According to Greek myth, beautiful Queen Helen ran off with a prince called Paris to the powerful city of Troy (in what is now Turkey). Her husband, Menelaus, and other Greek kings followed with a huge army.

They besieged Troy, but the Trojans wouldn't give in. After ten long years of fighting, everyone just wanted the war to be over.

Finally, one Greek hero, Odysseus, thought of a clever plan to defeat the Trojans. First he had to go on a secret mission. There was a prophecy that Troy would not fall as long as it had the Palladium, a sacred stone belonging to the goddess Athena. The stone was in a temple under the city. Odysseus disguised himself as an old beggar and slipped through the gates into Troy. Nobody looked twice at him, but Odysseus was taking note of all the landmarks in the city.

Then Helen recognized Odysseus, even with his disguise. When Odysseus told her what he wanted, she showed him where the stone was because she too was fed up with the long war. Odysseus smuggled the Palladium out of the city.

It was time for the second part of his plan. The Greeks built a huge wooden horse, big enough to hold a band of soldiers. Some soldiers hid inside the horse, and others hid nearby, while the Greeks pretended to sail their ships away.

One man was left, a spy called Sinon. He told the Trojans that he had been beaten and left behind. The wooden horse, he said, was an offering to the gods for a safe voyage home. The Trojans took the horse inside the gates. Can you guess what happened? The prophecy really did come true. Late that night when everyone was asleep, tired out from partying, the Greeks attacked. Poor Trojans—for ten years they had held out against the Greeks, and then their city was destroyed in one night!

HEY! WHERE'S EVERYBODY GOING?

Trojan horse

RUTHLESS ROMANS

The Romans believed they were descended from the Trojans. And *they* weren't going to be beaten by anyone. Rome was full of spies. Noble families had their own, and the Roman army used spies when Rome was at war with other powerful states.

Rome fought a series of wars against the African city of Carthage from 272 to 146 BCE. The Carthaginian general, Hannibal, had spies everywhere. Any spy who made a mistake was in big trouble. Hannibal once ordered the execution of one unlucky spy who sent him to the wrong city (which had a name that sounded like the right city).

On the Roman side, General Scipio Africanus had his own spying methods. He sent officers to the Carthaginian camp to discuss a truce, but the Romans took along some slaves—only they were really officers in disguise. There was one officer who might have been recognized, so he was beaten in front of the enemy, as if he really were a slave.

DO YOU THINK ANYONE WILL RECOGNIZE ME NOW?

They knew the Carthaginians wouldn't believe an officer would let himself be beaten in public like that. The Roman soldiers and their "slaves" looked carefully at the layout of the camp. They attacked that night —and won.

Years later, Roman emperors had their own spies. Some of them, the *frumentarii*, started out as supply sergeants. No one suspected supply sergeants of spying, because they had to travel around to buy supplies for the army. They became a sort of secret police, spying on those who might be against the emperor. They were hated and feared by the people.

Roman emperors believed they needed their spies to survive. Did the spies help? Well . . . only a quarter of the emperors died of old age or illness. The rest were *murdered*.

READ IT, JULIUS!

Julius Caesar was a great Roman general who wrote books about his military adventures. Caesar used spies to gather information, and he made sure messages were coded, in case his spies were captured. But then he made a crucial mistake. Some members of the Senate, the government of Rome, planned to kill him. A few minutes before the Senate meeting, one of his spies handed Caesar a list of the men who were plotting to assassinate him . . . *but he didn't read it!* Julius Caesar was stabbed to death in 44 BCE.

2

WHAT YOU SEE iS WHAT YOU GET—NOT!

Secret agents have to know more than the language and details of the country they are spying in. They have to know how to act like the locals so they are not noticed. If they are "sleeper agents," they have to live in the place where they're spying, as ordinary members of that community, till they are ordered into action.

They need a range of old clothes and good clothes so they blend in. If they are on the run, they might cut their hair, wear glasses, grow a beard, or stain their teeth. In some cases, they might even have plastic surgery before they go on a mission.

In World War II, British secret agents slipped into France wearing French-styled clothes and maybe a Swiss watch. They cut off British clothing labels and had their dental fillings changed to match French ones. Over the centuries, spies have worn all sorts of disguises. Men have disguised themselves as women, and women have dressed as men. One white woman spy, Sarah Emma Edmonds, disguised herself as an African-American man!

THE SPY IN A PINK NIGHTIE

A hundred years ago, when ladies wore elegant long dresses and hats with veils to protect them from the sun, a lovely young woman was holidaying on a yacht off the coast of France. Each day she would paint charming scenes of French boats, and then the yacht would sail on to the next harbor. But if you looked closer, you might have noticed that Miss Edith Murphy's shoulders were rather broad. And her gloved hands were large—most unusual for a well-bred lady of 1903.

In fact, Miss Edith was an Australian spy working for the British, and "she" was really a man! Herbert Dyce Murphy was painting watercolors to record information about the French navy and railways.

Herbert Dyce Murphy was born in Melbourne in 1879. He studied at Oxford University in England, and in his summer holidays he worked as a sailor. But he had been spotted in a university play, in a female role. He acted so well that a man from British Intelligence who was in the audience asked him to work as a spy in Europe, disguised as a woman. The British government wanted someone to check out the condition of French and Belgian railways. If the French were planning for war, the railways would be used to carry soldiers and equipment. A man snooping around the trains would be more suspicious than a young lady painting pictures.

Herbert was short of money, so he said yes. He learned how to act like a girl and grew his hair long, which was safer than wearing a wig. As a spy, he had a chaperone—an older woman who traveled with him—as all respectable young ladies did in those days.

The chaperone's real job was to make sure nobody caught "Edith" putting on his disguise or shaving. Herbert had some strange experiences during his spying career. Once he had to take over the wheel in an emergency on board a ship—in a pink, see-through nightgown! Luckily, the crew knew his secret. The King of England, Edward VII, fell in love with "Edith," and a young French officer proposed marriage. Another time, Herbert was chased around a train by a German officer.

Eventually, Herbert grew tired of having to live as a girl and retired from spying. He returned to working at sea and sailed on an Australian expedition to the Antarctic with famous explorer Douglas Mawson. He retired to a small town near Melbourne. There, he invited children to spend their summer holidays with him and passed the evenings telling them of his adventures.

FRENCH FRILLS AND RUSSIAN ROYALTY

Herbert Dyce Murphy wasn't the only cross-dressing male spy. In 1755, a pretty young woman left Paris on her way to the court of Empress Elizabeth of Russia. "She" was the Chevalier d'Eon, an excellent swordsman, who had played at dressing as a woman at parties to see if he could get away with it. King Louis XV of France wanted to re-establish contact with Russia without the British knowing, and Chevalier d'Eon agreed to be his spy. A woman had a better chance of surviving this mission, as she was less likely to be suspected of spying. Chevalier d'Eon's mission to have Empress Elizabeth sign a treaty with France was successful, and he left for England. But in England he became a double agent, working for both the British secret service and the French. When he refused to come home, he was paid off by the French on the condition that he wear women's clothes for the rest of his life. They thought he couldn't do them any harm as a woman, but perhaps Chevalier d'Eon was happier wearing women's clothes.

3

BELLE, BET, AND HARRiET: WOMEN UNDERCOVER

During the American Civil War (1861 to 1865), the northern Union states were at war with the southern Confederate states.

One of the reasons for this war was slavery. The South had slaves, the North didn't. The slaves were the descendants of African people kidnapped for the slave trade. They wanted freedom, so many of them wanted the Northern army to win. Slaves made good spies because their masters didn't think of them as people. Secrets were discussed in front of them as if they were invisible.

Women from both sides also spied. Nobody paid much attention to them either—a bad mistake! Harriet Tubman was a very brave woman who had smuggled many slaves to freedom before the war. She became a spy, disguising herself as a field hand or farmwife while organizing spy networks for the Northern army. Harriet had been a slave herself before escaping to freedom, and if she had been caught, she would have died horribly.

THE DOUBLE-CROSS-DRESSING SPY

Like other white women at this time, Sarah Emma Edmonds disguised herself as a man to fight for the Northern army under the name "Frank Thompson." When a spy was needed for a mission in Virginia, she disguised herself as a *male* slave. She wore a wig and colored her skin, then joined a group of Southern slaves who were building defense fortifications in Yorktown. When the dye started to come off her skin, she explained that she was turning white because her mother was a white woman!

She then got herself the job of carrying water around the Southern camp so she could listen to soldiers' conversations and check out the fortifications. One night, Sarah (still disguised as a man) was sent to take supper to the guards and was startled to be handed a gun. Some of the guards had been shot, and the slaves had to replace them. Sarah took the gun and slipped away to report the information about the Southern fortifications to her own army.

Not many spies in the Civil War were trained. Often a general only had to buy a newspaper from the other side to find out the enemy's plans. Cracking the enemy code was sometimes as easy as reading the washing.

Reading the washing . . . ?

SUDS AND SIGNALS

The Dabneys, a married African-American couple, escaped from slavery and found their way to the Northern army's camp, on one side of the Rappahannock River in Virginia. Mr. Dabney was fascinated by the army's flag signaling system and asked many questions. He got the hang of it, and then he and his wife made a plan.

Mrs. Dabney went across the river and got a job as a laundress, washing clothes at the headquarters of a Southern general. Not long after, Mr. Dabney began to pass on accurate information to Northern officers about the Southern army's movements. The officers were amazed. They asked, "How do you *do* it without ever leaving the camp?"

Mr. Dabney took them to the riverbank and showed them. Across the river, Mrs. Dabney was hanging clothes on the line. The Dabneys had worked out their own code. Each piece of clothing had a meaning. Even the way it was hung told a story.

"CRAZY BET"

One Southern woman, Elizabeth Van Lew, found a
way to help the Northern army. She had been taught
in a Quaker school, and the Quakers were firmly
against slavery. Elizabeth freed all her slaves and asked
one of them, Mary Bowser, to help her by working in
the home of the Southern president, Jefferson Davis.
Elizabeth pretended to be insane and became known in
her home town of Richmond, Virginia, as "Crazy Bet."
Using this disguise, she set up a network of couriers to
get information through to
the North.

While Crazy Bet was
sending her reports on what
the Southern army was
doing, using a secret code and
letters written in invisible
ink, her friend Mary Bowser
listened in to conversations
and memorized military
documents. She reported to

Crazy Bet by hiding documents in hollow eggs or in the false bottoms of dinner trays.

After the war, Elizabeth Van Lew was shunned by her neighbors as a traitor. Was she a traitor? Which is more important, being loyal to your country or acting according to your beliefs?

invisible letters

How do you make invisible ink? The simplest kind is lemon juice. You dip a toothpick or a small stick in the juice, write your message (in code, of course), and let it dry. To read your secret message you need to heat the paper. Use an iron to make your message visible—the letters will appear brown.

BOYISH BELLE BOYD

There were also several women doing their bit for the Southern army. One of these was Belle Boyd. She was captured a number of times but was always released. No one believed a woman could *possibly* be guilty of spying.

When Belle was 16, her town in West Virginia was occupied by Northern troops. She gathered information for the Southern army by mixing with the Northerners. When soldiers tried to break into her mother's home, she shot one of them. (This incident later appeared in a novel called *Gone With the Wind*.) She was tried in court for murder but was let off because it was done in self-defense.

Belle moved to another town, where she could be of more use collecting information about Northern troop movements. Disguised as a boy, she rode many miles to deliver the information to the Southern general, "Stonewall" Jackson, then continued with other

spy missions. When she became too well-known to continue spying, she got a job delivering important secret documents from the Southern states to Europe. On the way, the ship was captured, and Belle fell in love with a man from the other side, a Northern naval officer, Samuel Hardinge. He helped her escape to England and was dismissed from the navy for doing so. They married and settled in England, but Samuel died only a year later. After the war, Belle made a living as an actress and lecturer, telling people her story.

AERIAL SNOOPING

In these days of Earth-orbiting spy satellites that can "see" in amazing detail, it's hard to imagine anyone spying from hot-air balloons! Thaddeus Lowe, a scientist from the Northern states, got the idea when his balloon came down in South Carolina just after the American Civil War began—and he was arrested for spying. Later, he commanded a fleet of airships that reported on Southern troop movements and took aerial photos.

Modern spy satellites—usually called reconnaissance or recon satellites—can see detail on Earth to within a few feet, and some can even see through camouflage. Older satellites used to take photos and drop the film to the ground with tiny parachutes. Today's photos are digital, and computers can make three-dimensional images and even three-dimensional animations of the land below. Satellites travel over every spot on Earth twice a day!

HEY- I CAN SEE MY HOUSE!

4

SECRET SERViCE iN THE TWO WORLD WARS

In both World War I and World War II, many men and women risked their lives to get urgent military information through to their commanders. Some were trained to be spies; others were asked to spy because of their special knowledge or skills. But some people took up spying just for the money.

THE DANCING SPY

When we speak of a female
spy, we often call
her a "Mata Hari."
But the real Mata
Hari wasn't very good at
spying, and no one is sure who
she was working *for*. Her real
name was Margaretha Zelle
and she was famous as a dancer.
During World War I (1914–
1918), Mata Hari was asked to
spy for Germany. She decided
she could use the money.
Then she was offered a job spying for the French, who
were fighting the Germans. She agreed to do it, for
a million francs, but she was mistaken for another
German spy and was dragged off to England for
questioning. She said she was working for the French,
but the French spy agency denied it. Still, Mata Hari
was released and sent to Spain, where she may have

done more spying for the Germans. In 1917 she was arrested in France and shot. There's a story that she blew a kiss to the firing squad.

THE "WHITE MOUSE"

Nancy Wake was a special agent during World War II (1939–1945). She was born in New Zealand in 1912 and immigrated to Australia with her family when she was two years old. In the 1930s she went to Europe to work as a journalist. The Nazis had come to power in Germany, and when Nancy saw how cruelly they were treating people, especially Jews, she was furious.

In 1940 she married a Frenchman, Henri Fiocca. Six months later the Nazis invaded France, and Nancy joined the French Resistance. She helped British

airmen escape after they'd been shot down in France and smuggled food and messages to the French Resistance rebels. The Nazis called her the "White Mouse" because they couldn't catch her. Once, Nazis actually arrested her, but she managed to escape. She had to flee France and go to Britain. Nancy joined the Special Operations Executive (SOE) and trained in all aspects of fighting and spying. She was parachuted back into France, where she organized air-drops of weapons, clothes, and food and kept radio messages going back to SOE headquarters.

After the war, she went back to France to find out what had happened to her husband. He had been tortured and killed by the Nazis. She received

many medals from different countries. The film *Charlotte Gray* is based on her adventures.

SZABO SABOTAGES

Nancy Wake survived World War II, but Violette Szabo didn't. She was born in 1921, grew up in England, and married a Frenchman, Etienne Szabo. Etienne was killed fighting in North Africa, and Violette vowed to fight those who had taken her husband's life. She went to train with the SOE so she could work with the French Resistance against the Germans. She was very good at shooting, but her trainers were worried because she spoke French with an English accent. If she were noticed and taken prisoner by the Nazis, then other people's lives would be in danger. Still, she was parachuted into France, where she helped reorganize a Resistance network that the Germans had destroyed. On her second mission, in 1944, she and her comrade, Jacques Dufour, were ambushed by Nazis when they were sabotaging telegraph lines. Violette, who was wounded and exhausted, urged Jacques to escape while she fired at the enemy. The Nazis captured and tortured her, but she revealed nothing. She was executed at the Ravensbrück concentration camp in Germany. A book, *Carve Her Name With Pride*, tells her story.

CLOAK-AND-DAGGER SPIES

In World War II, Special Operations agents were taught how to use guns and explosives, as well as Morse code and the art of disguise. They could blow up a bridge, derail a train, stop an enemy car, or kill with their bare hands. They could send and decode messages, make invisible ink, and even get out of a pair of handcuffs with a piece of thin wire and a pencil. Once they were fully trained, they'd be parachuted into enemy territory.

If an agent was captured and questioned by the Nazis, he or she had to try not to give away information for at least 48 hours so that other agents or Resistance fighters could cover their tracks.

ONLY FIVE MORE HOURS AND I START TALKING

THE OIL SALESMAN

Not all World War II spies were women. One man who risked his life to get vital information for the countries fighting the Germans (the Allies) was Eric Erickson.

Eric grew up in the United States but went to live in Sweden. He wasn't a professional spy; he was an oil salesman. The American ambassador to Sweden asked Eric to go to Germany to find out about German oil refineries and where they kept their oil supplies. Eric could travel there on business, to buy oil, and nobody would suspect he was spying.

First, though, he had to win the trust of the enemy. Eric put pictures of Hitler in his office. He began speaking openly in favor of the Nazis and argued with his friends and family. They all thought he was a traitor. He persuaded Prince Carl Gustav, the Swedish king's nephew, to pretend to be a Nazi supporter too, so the prince could help him if he got into trouble.

The plan worked well. Heinrich Himmler, head of German state security, gave him written permission to go wherever he wanted in Germany to buy oil for Sweden.

At that time, Germany had plenty of oil to spare. Eric memorized the locations and layout of the oil stores.

Travelers in wartime Germany often had to share rooms in overcrowded hotels. Eric was terrified that he would talk in his sleep, so he took tablets to stay awake. He was helped by other spies, including a woman who became his girlfriend—but she was captured. Eric was invited by the Nazis to watch the execution of a group of spies, including his girlfriend. He was heartbroken, but he continued his work. His luck ran out when a man who had known him before the war spotted him and went to a phone booth to report his suspicions to the police. To save himself, Eric had to kill the man.

Now he had to flee! Prince Carl Gustav sent an official message saying that he must return to Sweden immediately.

The information that Eric brought back helped the American army destroy German oil supplies. Without oil, the Nazis couldn't run their tanks, trucks, and jeeps. By 1945, they had to use horses and oxen to haul their vehicles!

A film was made about Eric, *The Counterfeit Traitor*, based on a book of the same name.

Leave the parcel behind the third tree to the right of the seat. _Tonight!_

DEAD DROP

How do people with secret sneaky business swap messages (or money) when they can't risk being seen together? They plan a "dead drop."

First they need a drop location:

"Leave the money in a parcel under the bridge. Wrap it in a black plastic bag and cover it with leaves."

Then they need signals:

"My signal: one vertical piece of tape on the street sign means I am ready to receive your parcel. Your signal: one horizontal piece of tape when the drop is filled. My signal: one vertical piece of tape when I have received your parcel."

A simple plan—no one would notice the exchange—but can spies ever trust the people they are working for?

SPOOKSPEAK

*Here are some spy words from the
International Spy Museum website.*

Babysitter: Bodyguard.

Bagman: An agent who pays spies and bribes authorities.

Bang and Burn: Demolition and sabotage operations.

Birdwatcher: British Intelligence term for a spy.

Black Bag Job: Secret entry into a home or office to steal or copy materials.

Brush Pass: A brief encounter where something is passed between a case officer and agent.

Chicken Feed: Convincing, but not critical, intelligence knowingly provided to an enemy intelligence agency by an agent or a double agent.

BRUSH PASS

Cobbler: A spy who creates false passports, visas, diplomas, and other documents.

Counterintelligence: Spy-catching.

Cryptography: The art of writing or breaking code.

Dangle: A person who approaches an intelligence agency with the intent of being recruited to spy against his or her own country.

Discard: An agent whom an intelligence agency will permit to be detected and arrested so as to protect more valuable agents.

Ears Only: Material too secret to commit to writing.

Executive Action: Assassination.

Eyes Only: Documents that may be read but not discussed.

Floater: A person used one time, occasionally, or even unknowingly for an intelligence operation.

Hospital: Russian intelligence term for prison.

L-Pill: A poison pill used by operatives to commit suicide.

Mole: An agent of one organization sent to penetrate another intelligence agency by gaining employment.

Music Box: A secret radio.

Pig: Russian intelligence term for traitor.

Pocket Litter: Items in a spy's pocket (receipts, coins, theater tickets, etc.) that add authenticity to his or her identity.

Rolled-up: When an operation goes bad and an agent is arrested.

Shoe: A false passport or visa.

The spookspeak presented here is drawn from fact and fiction, from agencies and authors around the world and throughout time. For more on the language of espionage, go to http://www.spymuseum.org/ educate/loe.asp

5

SPY GADGETS AND SECRET WEAPONS

Have you ever wondered if all the tricky devices they have in spy movies could possibly exist? Who could make those tiny cameras disguised as wristwatches, or hollow coins with "microdot" film hidden inside? What about guns hidden in a ring or a lipstick?

Actually, some of the technology used in espionage is every bit as weird as what you see in the movies. Wristwatch cameras and hollow coins are still used. The spy agency of the Soviet Union, the KGB, did issue a lipstick gun in the 1960s. It had only one bullet and was designed to be used in an emergency, so the spy could escape. And microdot cameras were very useful. You could take photos so tiny that they fit into a period at the end of a sentence. All you had to do then was write a letter or a postcard and insert the photo, and it would be enlarged at spy headquarters.

SNEAKY TRICKS

Spying went on around the clock, and darkness gave spies good cover. Where a flashlight or candle would give a spy away, night-vision goggles meant spies could watch people in their rooms or read secret documents by the light of a cigarette. Battery-powered night-vision goggles have a light intensifier inside that makes dim light much brighter.

In World War II, when SOE agents arrived in Asia by boat, they wore special shoes with rubber soles that would leave barefoot footprints in the sand. The local people often didn't wear shoes, and bootprints in the sand would have been very suspicious.

The SOE had another cunning plan. They bought dead rats and filled them with explosives. The rats were placed on the piles of coal that were to be shoveled into furnaces in Germany. Boom! But the exploding rats were discovered. The Germans were pretty impressed and kept looking for other exploding rodents, just in case.

BUGS

A "bug" is something used to hear and record information secretly. Sometimes it really is disguised as an insect. A flying "bug" that will stick to a wall has already been invented. The American intelligence agency, the CIA, had a dragonfly bug, which looked real but couldn't stay on course when it was windy.

The government of the former Soviet Union gave the American embassy in Moscow a beautifully carved wooden reproduction of the Great Seal of the US. This was displayed proudly . . . until it was discovered to be a listening device! For seven years, every word in the American ambassador's office was overheard. Still, the Soviet embassy in Washington was probably bugged too, by the CIA.

PLAINCLOTHES PIGEONS

The first "spy gadget" was probably the carrier pigeon, which was used for centuries to carry vital messages during wartime. During World War II, carrier pigeons were still being used to carry messages in case radio contact failed. In one case, a pigeon saved the day by carrying urgent information through Japanese fire to American army headquarters. The pigeon, known as Number 879, won a medal!

In the 1970s, the CIA found another use for birds: carrying a camera to take aerial photos. It took a while to get this particular "gadget" right, though. The first camera-carrying pigeon was overloaded and couldn't fly far enough to be any use.

$7 MILLION IN ONE NIGHT

In World War II, the beautiful and intelligent actress Hedy Lamarr was married to an arms dealer who worked for the Nazis. She left him and escaped to America. There she applied to join the National Inventors Council and was told to help raise money for war bonds by offering kisses! (She raised $7 million by selling kisses for $25,000 each!) Then Hedy and musician George Antheil developed an idea for "frequency-hopping" radio signals that would prevent the enemy from blocking radio-guided torpedoes. The idea wasn't used during the war, but an advanced version—spread-spectrum technology—has been used in cell phones, wireless Internet, cordless phones, and military communication systems.

TiGER POO AND TiNNY FiSH

Another listening device, developed for use in Asia, was a fake pile of tiger droppings. It came in handy for Americans trying to work out the movements of enemy troops on jungle trails during the Vietnam War. Who, after all, was going to check out a smelly pile of poo?

UH OH

IT LOOKS LIKE THIS AND WE'RE NOT GOING TO REST UNTIL WE FIND IT.

It's sometimes important to collect water samples around nuclear plants in enemy territory to find out what they're doing with nuclear materials, and what could be better for this than a fish? Not a real fish, of course, but the CIA's robot catfish. This catfish

looked so real that it even fooled other animals.
How surprised predators must have been, after biting
into a juicy catfish, to find it was hard metal!

THE SHOWMAN WHO SAVED A CITY

As well as gadgets, there are tricks to confuse the
enemy. There once was a famous stage magician, Jasper
Maskelyne, who joined the British army in 1939, when
Britain went to war against Germany. He wanted to be
an army engineer. Instead, he was sent to North Africa
to entertain the troops.

In 1941, Jasper got the chance to use his skills for
a hugely important task. Rommel, the general leading
Germany's army in Africa, wanted to attack the British

troops in Egypt. His spy planes were scouting the skies over Alexandria and the Suez Canal. Jasper led a group of experts known as the Magic Gang, whose job was to fool the German aerial spies.

They built a copy of Alexandria harbor in a nearby bay so that the Germans wouldn't bomb the real Alexandria. They made fake buildings, a phony lighthouse, even fake anti-aircraft guns, which gave off impressive flashes to make the attackers think they were being shot at. Revolving mirrors near the Suez Canal made huge spinning lights so that German bombers couldn't find the canal.

Jasper Maskelyne's biggest success was in 1942, when the Germans in Egypt were expecting a British attack but didn't know where or when it would happen.

The Magic Gang built 2000 fake tanks from painted canvas and wood, while 1000 real British tanks were somewhere else, disguised as trucks. The Magic Gang also built a false railway line, which the Germans thought was to transport troops. German pilots saw the British busily building a (fake) water pipe, as if to supply the troops along the way. From what they could see, the German commanders were certain the British wouldn't be able to attack before November. They were wrong. The British attacked in late October and from an unexpected direction. Thousands of German soldiers died, and the German campaign in Africa was wrecked. Jasper Maskelyne helped to change the course of World War II.

Jasper Maskelyne told his story in a book called *Magic: Top Secret*, but after the war there was no longer work for a stage magician. He died years later in Kenya.

CRACKING THE CODE: ENIGMA

Spies send messages in code so the enemy can't read them. Cracking codes was a key part of the war effort for the British and their allies. During World War II, Britain employed many people as cryptographers. They worked at a place called Bletchley Park, trying to translate German messages. Huge computers, called Colossus, were built to help. One of their great achievements was cracking the Germans' Enigma code.

THE ENIGMA MACHINE

THE CODE-BREAKING COMPUTER

The Enigma machine looked like a typewriter with some add-ons and worked like a basic computer, turning messages into code or translating codes back into readable messages. The German navy had used it for its secret communications since 1925. By the time World War II began in 1939, the British knew the machine existed. The trouble was they didn't have the codebooks and manuals they needed to understand how it actually worked. It wasn't just a matter of finding out what a single message said, because next time the machine would have been reset to a new code. The same combination of letters in the next message might mean something completely different.

In 1940, the British had a stroke of luck. Their ship *Griffin* captured some papers from a German navy ship disguised as a fishing trawler. The German crew threw two bags of papers overboard, and *Griffin*'s gunner dived overboard to get them. He managed to grab one, while the other sank.

The documents in the bag had a few days' worth of useful information in them, enabling the Bletchley cryptographers to read German messages for those days. It wasn't enough, though. The cryptographers had to know how the Germans changed their settings.

The Germans made one mistake: they used real fishing trawlers to deliver weather reports to their navy. The navy then replied using Enigma. That meant the trawlers had to have Enigma machines—and codebooks—on board so they could translate the navy's messages.

In June 1941, the British destroyer HMS *Tartar* found a German weather ship north of Iceland. *Tartar*'s gun crew fired—but carefully avoided hitting the target. The German crew abandoned ship, leaving the British free to board. The British didn't bother taking the Enigma machine, but they did make off with their papers. A naval intelligence officer, Allon Bacon, sorted through the papers and finally found what he wanted: a diagram with instructions for changing settings inside the Enigma machine. The puzzle was closer to being solved. Later, codebooks were taken from a German submarine, and cryptographers could set to work cracking codes.

After the war, the British government destroyed the Colossus in order to keep the work done at Bletchley Park secret.

6

COOL CATS AND COLD WAR DiSASTERS

Imagine people chatting at a cocktail party at a government embassy. A glossy cat is slinking around people's legs as they drink and talk. Nobody takes much notice of him, but that cruising cat is more than he seems . . . .

In the 1960s, someone in the CIA had the idea of a cat "spy." Operation Acoustic Kitty was a plan to wire a cat for sound. They would implant a microphone into a cat and an antenna in his tail and then train him to obey orders.

It was a costly project and a big mistake. Anyone who has ever owned a cat knows it won't do *anything* it doesn't want to do. When the cat got hungry, he went for a snack. If a female cat wandered past, he went after her. Then, when the CIA sent him off to spy on people in the park, poor Acoustic Kitty was knocked over by a car on his first day. A CIA agent rushed over to retrieve the equipment from his insides.

This is only one of the crazy ideas dreamed up by spy agencies during the 1950s and 1960s—a period known as the Cold War. Up until a few years ago, the CIA's files from this time were top secret. No one was allowed to see them. Now the files are open and they tell us some interesting things.

SO, WHAT **WAS** THE COLD WAR?

During World War II, the United States and the USSR (now the Commonwealth of Independent States, including Russia) fought together to defeat Nazi Germany. But the Americans and the Russians were never on friendly terms. The USSR was communist and the Americans thought communism was anti-democratic and dangerous. After World War II, both countries spied on each other and stockpiled weapons in case the other side attacked. This armed truce was known as the Cold War because no shots were actually fired. The most famous modern spy stories happened during this time.

The race to get into space was a part of this "war." The USSR got there first, in 1957, with a satellite called *Sputnik.* Much later, both sides sent up satellites to spy on each other from space.

THE OLD EXPLODING CIGAR TRICK

In the late 1950s and early 1960s, the CIA was trying to defend democracy from any communist threat. Fidel Castro was president of the communist country of Cuba, which is right on the United States' doorstep. The CIA wanted to get rid of Castro.

Castro was famous for his bushy beard and his fondness for cigars. Both were used against him. There was a silly plan to make a powder that would cause his beard to fall out. Another plan was to send him an exploding cigar. We don't know if the CIA got these anywhere near him, but Castro didn't lose his beard. The next bright idea was to pump a drug into a studio where Castro was to give an interview, making him appear silly. That didn't work either. The "Make Castro Look Like a Fool" project was a flop.

The CIA got serious then, with a plan to kill him. Castro loved scuba diving, so someone thought, "Aha! Let's give him a poisoned wetsuit!" But the American

BEFORE

AFTER

EXTREME MAKEOVER

diplomat who was supposed to deliver it wisely decided his country couldn't afford the trouble it would cause. He handed over a clean wetsuit instead.

So the CIA didn't succeed in killing or embarrassing Fidel Castro.

SPOOKY IDEAS

The USSR was Enemy Number 1 as far as the CIA was concerned. The agency tried to use California psychics to tell them what was going on there. Why send spies into danger when mind readers could close their eyes and "watch" another country without leaving home?

Well, in the test run, the psychic who was asked to "see" a particular place in Russia got the details wrong.

The CIA did another test on its own employees to see if drugs would help in questioning captured enemies. But the drug could make people hallucinate, and one poor CIA worker jumped out of a window.

THE CAMBRIDGE DOUBLE AGENTS

The Cold War was a scary time whether you lived in the USSR or in America or Britain. Both sides were stockpiling weapons and making atomic bombs, and war was a real possibility. People believed spies were *everywhere*, and there *was* a lot of spying going on.

In Britain, the "Cambridge spies" were recruited at England's Cambridge University in the 1930s. These men were double agents, spying for the USSR while working for British Intelligence. In fact, one of them, Kim

WHO IS THIS MAN ???

Philby, was high up in Britain's MI6 agency, in charge of spying on Soviet spies when he was giving information about Britain and the US to Russia. Kim Philby escaped to Russia in the 1950s.

EVERY MAN FOR HiMSELF: THE ROSENBERGS

There was such a fear of communism in America in the 1950s that sometimes innocent people were accused of spying. Among these were Julius and Ethel Rosenberg, a married couple who were charged with having sold secrets before the Cold War began. They would not admit to spying for the USSR, even though they had two young children, and a confession might have saved their lives.

Julius and Ethel claimed to be innocent, but they were sent to the electric chair in 1953.

People accused of working for the USSR couldn't just confess; they had to accuse someone else if they wanted to receive a lighter sentence. Ethel Rosenberg's brother, David Greenglass, was a soldier. When he was charged with giving nuclear secrets to the USSR, he said Ethel and her husband had been involved. Julius Rosenberg insisted he knew nothing about it. He had been a communist before the war, but it wasn't illegal then.

Some Russian files have been translated that suggest that Julius, at least, might have been spying for the USSR at one time, but had probably not committed the crime for which he was executed. Ethel was accused in order to force Julius to pass on more names of communist spies.

Later, David Greenglass admitted he had accused his sister to save his own wife and himself.

DON'T TRUST ANYONE...

After World War II, Germany was divided. West Germany was a democracy and East Germany was communist.

In East Germany, many ordinary people were encouraged to spy on their family and neighbors, reporting any "suspicious" behavior to the Stasi, the secret police. The Stasi kept secret records on a huge number of people. In the two years before Germany was finally reunited in 1991, the Stasi shredded these records to remove the evidence of who had been spying. There were 16,000 sacks (180 kilometers or 112 miles) of shredded paper! Now 250 sacks of paper have been reconstructed—by hand! Computer technology might help finish off the job, which otherwise will take 400 years!

The rest of it must be here somewhere!

7

BEST-SELLiNG SPiES

Many writers of spy stories had experience as spies
or intelligence officers. One of the first spy thrillers,
The Thirty-Nine Steps (1915), was written by an
intelligence officer, John Buchan. Graham Greene,
author of many exciting novels, including *The Quiet
American*, was working for British Intelligence in
the Cold War era. Most famous of all was writer
Ian Fleming, the creator of the daring agent 007,
James Bond. Ian Fleming worked for British Naval
Intelligence during World War II.

THE SPY WHO DIED AT DINNER

Christopher Marlowe (1564–1593) was a playwright who lived in London at the same time as William Shakespeare. Marlowe was almost certainly a spy working for Francis Walsingham, spymaster to Queen Elizabeth I.

The queen had a lot of enemies. Some of her own people thought her cousin, Mary, Queen of Scots, should be queen. Elizabeth needed clever spies to protect her position as queen.

When Francis Walsingham died, there were things certain people didn't want the new spymaster to know and were afraid Christopher Marlowe might reveal.

Marlowe's spying came to an end when he was stabbed in the eye in a pub brawl. His killer, Ingram Frizer, claimed they had argued over the bill. More likely

he killed Marlowe to keep him quiet. Ingram Frizer
pleaded self-defense and only spent 28 days in
prison for the murder.
Maybe Christopher
Marlowe
should have
stuck to
writing drama.

CODENAME ASTREA

Someone who was definitely sorry she hadn't stuck to
writing drama was Aphra Behn. Aphra had a romance
with a man called William Scot. They called themselves
Astrea and Celedon, after the main characters of a
popular novel called *L'Astree*. These later came in
handy as spy codenames.

Aphra married a Dutch merchant called Behn
in 1664, but he died the next year, the year England
went to war with the Dutch. By this time, William
Scot, Aphra's old love, was living in Holland. He had
given the British government important information

about the Dutch, but he had killed two British agents.
The British government thought he might be working
for the enemy as well.

In 1666, Aphra was sent to Holland to contact
William Scot and offer him a royal pardon if he agreed
to come back to the English side. William agreed.
He told her that the Dutch were planning a raid on
London up the Thames River. At great risk to her own
life, Aphra smuggled the information to England, but
the British government didn't act on it and the Dutch
raid went ahead. Aphra was furious. Even worse, she
was stuck in Holland until 1667, and she had to borrow
money to get home because her spymaster hadn't given
her any money for expenses. *Then* she was jailed in
London for being unable to pay her debts!

63

Eventually the government paid off her debts, but that was the end of Aphra Behn's spy career. She spent the rest of her life as a best-selling writer instead. Some of her books are still in print, and her plays are still being performed.

THE FATHER OF THE BRITISH SECRET SERVICE

Daniel Defoe took up spying because he was broke. He had spent all his money in 1685 supporting a rebellion by the Duke of Monmouth against the king, and he was lucky not to be executed when the rebellion failed. Daniel became a journalist and wrote an article mocking the government . . . and he was put into jail. After his release, he wrote to a powerful politician with a proposal for a secret service. Daniel would run it, and teams of spies would travel around England reporting anyone who might be a danger to the government. The idea was a success, and Daniel traveled England posing as a merchant called Alexander Goldsmith.

Daniel was also the editor of a Scottish newspaper

while he was working for the English government. Through his writing he managed to undermine a movement to get the Scottish royal family back into power in England.

By 1720, Daniel was writing popular stories and making a good living, so he quit his spy job. He wrote his famous story *Robinson Crusoe* at this time.

THE PEN IS MIGHTIER THAN THE SWORD

But he was too much of a miser to pay off his debts and spent the rest of his life on the run from people to whom he owed money. Nobody came to his funeral.

POPOV THE SPY

"So, what can you tell me about Popov?" asked the British Naval Intelligence official.

The man in the gray suit read from his files. "Dusko Popov is a Yugoslav businessman," he said. "He likes wine and women and fast cars. The Germans wanted him to be a spy for them. He accepted. Then he came to us and offered to be a double agent. He could bring in a lot of valuable information."

"Then let's accept his offer," said the official, whose name was Ian Fleming.

After the war, Fleming wrote a series of thrilling adventures about a secret agent named James Bond, which later became hugely successful films. It's possible that James Bond was inspired by the agent Dusko Popov. Popov was very good at spying and gathering information. It's too bad the Americans didn't listen to

his warning that the Japanese were planning to bomb Pearl Harbor in Hawaii, where there were many US warships and planes. The course of World War II would have been very different if the US Pacific Fleet hadn't been attacked on December 7, 1941. Immediately after the attack, the US, which had been neutral, decided to join the Allies in the war against Japan and Germany.

8

CYBER-SPYiNG

The heads of spy agencies around the world must
have been thrilled when computers were invented.
For centuries, they'd had to get their information the
hard way—by getting people to break in, pay bribes,
and copy secret documents or smuggle them out.
Now, with computers and computer networks, they
could . . . well . . . get people to burgle, bribe, and make
copies. But the spies didn't
have to leave home to do it.
No more running the risk
of being taken prisoner or
being forced to say
who'd sent them.

All they needed now was a computer, a phone line, and a lot of talent. The age of the computer hacker had arrived.

SO, WHAT DOES A HACKER DO?

Think of a hacker as a sort of burglar who sits at home, breaks into other people's computers, and helps himself to information. If the computers have been networked (linked together), the hacker can poke around in all the computers in the network or even sabotage the system. Hackers can also use viruses to infiltrate networks all over the world.

Most hackers are computer nerds who like to show off their skills. Sometimes they are just thieves, out to steal money from bank accounts or steal secrets for a competing business. And then there are the spies . . . .

THE "HANOVER HACKER"

In 1986, Clifford Stoll had a job programming computers at a university laboratory in Berkeley, California. In those days the Internet existed, but only a few people used it for business. Personal computers were not as common as they are now, but universities, governments, and businesses were starting to use networks. Computer users had passwords but didn't yet understand how important it was to be careful with them.

One day, Cliff was asked to fix a small problem. The lab kept track of how much time and money was spent on computer use. Each time someone logged into the network, the cost was registered by an accounting program. A bill was 75 cents more than it should have been. Cliff expected to fix the problem very quickly.

Then he realized there was something strange about this "mistake." He tracked the 75 cents to a user whose log-in name was "Hunter," but "Hunter" wasn't on the lab's official list. Checking further, Cliff found that "Hunter" had been using the log-in account of a worker who was overseas and hadn't used the account in a year. The intruder had used the account to give himself "system manager" privileges, which meant he could not only look around the computer network for information, but could also make changes.

"Hunter" was definitely a hacker at work.

TRACK THE HACKER

For months, Cliff Stoll made a note of every "visit." He printed out everything the hacker typed into the network and even set his pocket pager to beep whenever the hacker was online. The hacker turned up at all sorts of strange times, so sometimes Cliff slept under his desk at the lab, much to his girlfriend's annoyance!

It would have been easy for Cliff to block the network against the intruder, but Cliff wasn't satisfied with that. If the hacker was blocked at the Berkeley lab, he'd find another entry point to the network, and then nobody would be able to track him. Cliff also knew that the hacker was using the Berkeley computers to get into other networks, including medical computers.

He could mess up records, and sick people's lives might be at risk if he wasn't stopped.

When he found out that the hacker was after military secrets, Cliff warned the FBI and CIA, America's two intelligence agencies. But neither was very alarmed. If no money was involved (except the 75 cents) and no actual damage had been done, then they didn't see it as their problem. Even the police weren't interested.

Eventually, with help from other computer experts, Cliff discovered that the phone calls connecting the hacker to the computer networks were coming from outside the US, from Hanover in West Germany. *Now* the CIA and FBI were interested. But they insisted on doing their own investigations and wouldn't tell Cliff what was happening.

Frustrated, Cliff continued on his own. Then his girlfriend, Martha, had a great idea: since the hacker wanted military secrets, why not give him false ones? They set up a phony military program called SDINET and invented a secretary who sent and received letters and documents with tempting military names for the program. The "secretary" invited official users to write to her and ask for copies.

Only a system manager could access SDINET, but ordinary system managers wouldn't be interested in military secrets. If anyone wrote, it would *have* to be the hacker. Cliff and Martha waited. Would their trap work?

Someone did reply! But the letter for documents came from an American address, not from Germany. Cliff contacted the CIA once more and got results.

Caught!

The hacker turned out to be a man called Markus Hess, one of a group who had been selling their stolen secrets to the KGB (the spy agency of the USSR). The KGB had asked a man working for them in the US to send the letter, to make sure SDINET was real.

GOTCHA!!!

Markus and his hacker pals were sentenced to two years in prison, and Cliff wrote a best-selling book about it all.

This happened in the days when hackers and viruses were rare. Now the Internet is used all around the world. We often hear about a new virus or someone caught hacking into banking or military networks across the world. And spy hackers are probably out there snooping for secrets . . . . The Internet has become a hacker heaven.

9

SHORT NINJA, TALL TALES

Silent, mysterious, fast-moving figures in black . . . leaping over rooftops and running up walls, a sword at your throat in an instant . . . . They disappear into the shadows, unnoticed, and overhear whispered secrets.

They are the ninja—warriors, spies, and assassins of Japan. Today, ninja arts (*ninjutsu*) are practiced by people who certainly don't lurk in the shadows, kill, or spy on enemies. "Ninja" comes from the Japanese phrase *shinobi-no-mono*, meaning "a person who hides his presence."

Extraordinary stories were told about the ninja. People thought they had supernatural powers, but they were just very, very good at what they did. The ninja probably encouraged the stories to make their enemies more afraid.

In one story, a dwarf ninja supposedly hid in the pit under an enemy lord's toilet and stabbed him when he went to relieve himself! Probably the lord died of a stroke, but it's easy to see how a story like this would spread. And it's only one of many tall tales about what these skilled fighters and spies could do.

Japanese warriors, the samurai, had a strict code of honor. Honor was challenging your enemy and fighting man-to-man in the open. Ninja behavior was the opposite. Ninja used ambushes and surprise attacks, and they often traveled in disguise. No wonder the samurai thought ninja dishonorable. They were tortured to death if they were caught.

Some Japanese warlords trained their own people as spies. Others hired ninja. After all, ninja were experts. If you were trapped in a fortress with enemies outside, you'd be glad to have ninja warriors with you because they could escape. A story of one besieged castle tells how, in the night, a ninja slipped out into the enemy camp, stole their flag, then flew it from the castle the next day to mock them.

STRAW DUMMIES AND NIGHTINGALE FLOORS

Ninjutsu was a family thing. Young ninja would be trained from childhood in the different techniques of fighting, running, hiding, swimming, and so on. They spent a lifetime perfecting their skills. No wonder the lords of warring clans took so much trouble to protect themselves!

In their castles they had traps, including squeaky floors called nightingale floors because they "sang" when someone stepped on them. The night guards would be on the scene immediately if they had unwelcome company.

Ninja were expert at disguise and did their homework. A ninja dressed as a farmer or priest would certainly know about farming or the priesthood, so his disguise would be convincing. He'd also be able to speak in different local accents to fool ferrymen when crossing rivers. Some ninja lived and worked inside an enemy fortress, but they were really "sleeper agents" who were called on when needed.

Ninja history goes back a long way. In the 1400s, there were around 70 ninja clans on the main Japanese island, Honshu. Ninja specialized in espionage. Their leaders were called *jonin*. The "middle men," who arranged jobs with the lords, were called *chunin*. The fighters were known as *genin*. They did the spying and fighting and often didn't know who their boss was.

Some ninja clans worked for just one noble family. The most famous ninja leader, Fuma Kotaro Nobuyuki, served a family called the Hojo, as his ancestors had done. He led about 200 ninja who fought, spied, and gathered information for the Hojo. Fuma Kotaro Nobuyuki's most famous action was a night attack on enemy forces, the Takeda. He had his men fake an attack, using horses with straw dummies as warriors. Meanwhile, the ninja smuggled themselves into the enemy camp, hiding along the sides of stolen Takeda horses. Then they attacked. In the darkness and confusion, the Takeda were killing each other instead of Fuma and his men.

This was the ninja way of doing things. Not "honorable," but intelligent!

NiNJA FACTS AND FiCTiON

Some people say the ninja

* wear black costumes
* throw star-shaped metal knives
* can walk through walls or "shape-shift"
* can become invisible
* can fly
* can come back as ghosts

Are these things true?

Well, there *is* a ninja uniform—trousers and hood in black, brown, or dark blue to help hide at night (or white in snowy weather)—but they didn't wear it while they were spying. Imagine a spy walking into an enemy stronghold in uniform! Mostly, ninja wore whatever was useful, including chain mail when they fought.

The star-knives, *shuriken*, were used to help ninja escape when they were being chased. They weren't always accurate but were useful to scare and delay the pursuer. Ninja carried other weapons to use in fights, such as knives and swords.

They couldn't walk through walls, of course. In Japanese houses, which had lots of gaps and crawl spaces, someone who knew the art of movement and how to blend in with the landscape could seem invisible. They couldn't fly, either, but they were great acrobats.

One ninja is supposed to have faked his own death so he could pretend to be a ghost. If people believe you're superhuman, they might well believe you're a ghost too!

Jiro's justice!

There's a story about Jiro, a young boy whose ninja father was killed by the Lord of Kuwana. Jiro was determined to avenge his father's death. First he made friends with the lord's son and went inside the house.

One day, Jiro hid in an old well and the lord's son thought he'd gone home. That night, Jiro climbed onto the roof and drilled a hole into the ceiling above the Lord of Kuwana. He lowered a silken thread through the hole and dripped poison down the thread—right into the snoring mouth of the lord! He went home, leaving the lord to die.

Kings, queens, and emperors have always had spies. Today, governments have intelligence agencies and big businesses steal information from each other. As long as people have secrets, there will be spies . . . .

GLOSSARY

ambushes surprise attacks from a hidden position

armed truce an agreement to stop fighting, but with each side keeping its weapons in case they start to fight again

authenticity something authentic is real, genuine

besieged surrounded by the enemy (in a castle or city) and unable to get out

crucial the most important, vital

communism a political system in which the government of the country runs everything and property is shared equally

democracy a political system (or country) in which the government is elected by the people

demolition destroying a building, bridge, etc.

diploma document from a school or university to show that the person has passed the final exams

espionage spying

hallucinate to see things that aren't there

journalist a person who writes for a newspaper or magazine

landmarks buildings or objects that stand out and help you find your way

reconnaissance checking out a place for the first time, or finding information of military use

sabotage to wreck or undermine tools, work, etc., on purpose (e.g., computer viruses are used to sabotage networks)

spymaster the boss of a spy agency

suicide to kill yourself (e.g., spies who don't want to be forced to speak may commit suicide)

viruses in the case of computers, programs written to wreck the working of the computer or a network, often sent by e-mail

visa special stamp on a passport that allows the owner to enter a particular country

WHERE TO FIND OUT MORE

Books

Ryan Hunter, *In Disguise! Stories of Real Women Spies*, Beyond Words, Hillsboro, OR, 2004

Richard Platt, *Spy*, Eyewitness Guide, Dorling Kindersley, London, 2000

Kate Walker and Elaine Argaet,
Spies in History,
Spies and Their Gadgets,
So You Want to Be a Spy,
Super Spies of World War I,
Super Spies of World War II,
Famous Spy Cases,
all in the Spies and Spying series, Smart Apple Media, North Mankato, MN, 2003

Websites

- www.bbc.co.uk/history/worldwars/

(the BBC is always good for general homework help)

- www.bletchleypark.org.uk

(has information about Enigma and Colossus, with links to other sites)

- www.cia.gov/cia/ciakids/index.shtml

(has all the spy gadget stuff in the "spy museum" section and even a "so you wanna be a spy" section)

- www.codesandciphers.org.uk
- www.spymuseum.org
- www.wikipedia.org

(a free online encyclopedia)

For teachers

Norman Polmor and Thomas Allen, *Spy Book; The Encyclopedia of Espionage*, 2nd ed., Random House, New York, 2004

Clifford Stoll, *The Cuckoo's Egg: Tracking a Spy through the Maze of Computer Espionage*, Pocket Books, New York, 2005

- www.home.netspeed.com.au/reguli/samhist.htm

(this URL will take teachers to an article about characters, both fictional and historical, mentioned in the TV series "The Samurai")

- www.nd.edu/~ndhpssum/Documents/TennysonSiegel-Enigma%20Lesson%20Plan.doc

INDEX

SUE BURSZTYNSKI saw her first spy
movie when she was eight. There was a family
rumor that her cousin had worked for military
intelligence, but Sue didn't follow in his footsteps.
Instead she writes books about monsters,
astronauts, archaeology, women scientists, and
wheels—and fiction books too. She works in a
school library and might be spotted at science
fiction conventions.

MItch Vane, CodenAMe: The Squid
becAuse of her use of black ink in many of her
illustrations. Specializes in identikit Pictures,
forgerY, and secret codes.

THANKS

I would like to thank Nikki White for advice on ninja; Bart Rutherford O'Connor for help on hackers; Anne Watling for checking the text; Gary Pearl, Joanne Davis, Fiona Ellem, and the students of Gandel Besen House, Dandenong West Primary School, and Charleville State School.

Sue Bursztynski

The publishers would like to thank the following for photographs used through the book:

istockphoto.com and photographers: Stefan Klein (torn paper, photo frames, and folder used throughout text); page i Rebecca Ellis (dragonfly); pages i, viii, 37 Edyta Pawlowska (magnifying glass); page viii Sue Colvil (Roman soldier); page 5 Maartje van Caspel (notebook computer); page 20 Dan Brandenburg (soldiers); page 28 Greg Nicholas (negative strip); page 34 George Cairns (meeting place); page 38 International Spy Museum, Washington DC (hollow coin); page 40 Clayton Hansen (dynamite); page 40 Kelly Resener (rat); page 51 James Hernandez (paw prints); page 57 Duncan Walker (mysterious man); pages 57, 74 Greg Nicholas (photo frame); page 74 Sean Locke (handcuffed man); page 82 José Manuel Ferrão (ninja); page 82 Slavolijub Pantelic (*shuriken*); page 83 Bryce Knoll (notepaper); page 84 Gergely Bényi (binoculars); the Library of Congress, Prints and Photographs Division, for photographs on page 16 Harriet Tubman [LC-USZ62-7816], page 23 Belle Boyd [LC-DIG-cwpbh-01991], page 28 Morse code operators [LC-USW3-035513-D and LC-USW3-035512-D], page 36 World War II poster [LC-USZC4-2793]; and the National Security Agency, USA, for the photographs on page 41 (US seal) and page 48 (the Enigma and the computer Bombe).